The Kirill Kaprizov Story

SMALL TOWN, BIG DREAMS

by Chad Israelson

illustrations
by Phil Juliano

Minneapolis, Minnesota

To my sons, Addison and Garrison, and
to all young sports fans and book lovers.

—Chad

For Emmy, Luca, and Marlo.

—Phil

Acknowledgments: I express gratitude to my wife, Beth Butterfield, for her many suggestions, proofreading, and support. I would also like to thank Ryan Jacobson and Lake 7 Creative, LLC, for the opportunity to collaborate on this project. —Chad

Edited by Ryan Jacobson
Proofread by Emily Beaumont
Fact-checked by Chris Zobin

ISBN: 978-1-960084-30-9
ebook: 978-1-960084-21-7

KIRILL KAPRIZOV'S CAREER STATISTICS

KONTINENTAL HOCKEY LEAGUE (KHL)

YEAR	TEAM	GAMES	GOALS	ASSISTS	POINTS	PLUS/MINUS
2014–15	Metallurg Novokuznetsk	31	4	4	8	-4
2015–16	Metallurg Novokuznetsk	53	11	16	27	-4
2016–17	Salavat Yulaev Ufa	49	20	22	42	9
2017–18	CSKA Moscow	46	15	25	40	22
2018–19	CSKA Moscow	57	30	21	51	34
2019–20	CSKA Moscow	57	33	29	62	32
Totals		**293**	**113**	**117**	**230**	**89**

NATIONAL HOCKEY LEAGUE (NHL)

YEAR	TEAM	GAMES	GOALS	ASSISTS	POINTS	PLUS/MINUS
2020–21	Minnesota Wild	55	27	24	51	10
2021–22	Minnesota Wild	81	47	61	108	27
2022–23	Minnesota Wild	67	40	35	75	4
Totals		**203**	**114**	**120**	**234**	**41**

SUPERSTAR SPORTS BIOGRAPHIES

The **Superstar Sports Biographies** aim to inspire children to read. Each picture book in the series presents the biography of a popular athlete from a professional sport such as baseball, basketball, football, or hockey. The biographies in this series are targeted to children ages 5 to 10 and are told as stories that are fun to read aloud. They include positive messages that promote character traits like integrity, kindness, and perseverance. Each children's book features full-color illustrations, includes the player's statistics, and is written by a sports fanatic.

Kirill Kaprizov was born on April 26, 1997, in the country of Russia. He lived in a small village. Winter was cold and snowy. That was good news for Kirill because he could play hockey.

By the time Kirill was four years old, he already loved the sport. "Some day, I'm going to play in the National Hockey League," he said.

Kirill might never play in the National Hockey League (NHL). The teams were all in the United States and Canada, on the other side of the world. How would they find Kirill in a small Russian village?

Still, Kirill's family supported him. His father drove him to the city of Novokuznetsk, over and over again, so Kirill could play hockey. The city was 35 miles away!

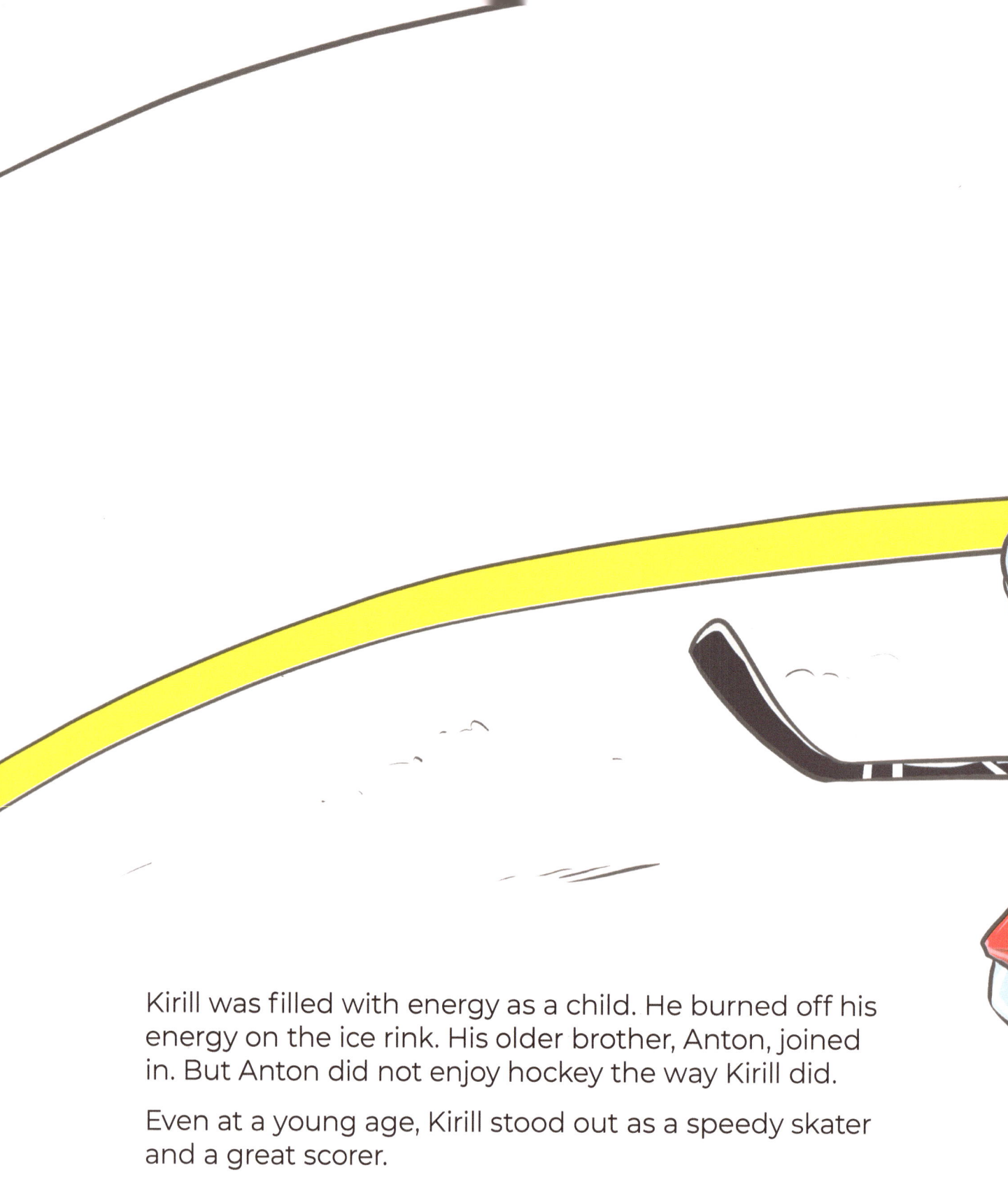

Kirill was filled with energy as a child. He burned off his energy on the ice rink. His older brother, Anton, joined in. But Anton did not enjoy hockey the way Kirill did.

Even at a young age, Kirill stood out as a speedy skater and a great scorer.

Kirill worked hard and kept getting better. After four years, his parents, Oleg and Natalya, made a big decision to help their son. They moved the family into the city. This allowed Kirill to practice and play more hockey.

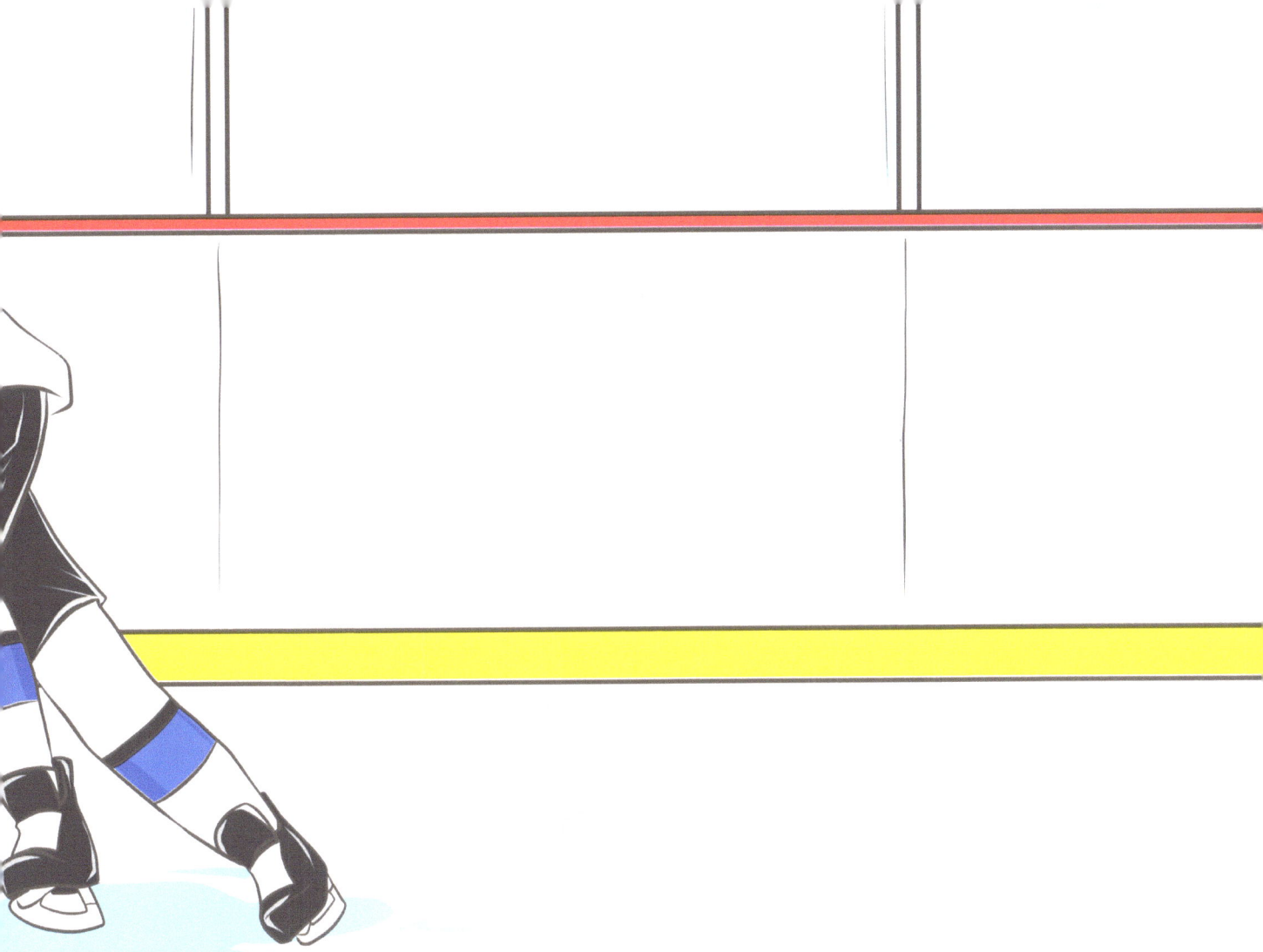

In 2013, at the age of 16, Kirill began playing in the Junior Hockey League. His team was the Kuznetskie Medvedi.

As one of the youngest players, Kirill ranked third on the team with 34 points. His coach said he was the "soul of the team."

A couple of years later, Kirill caught a lucky break. A scout from an NHL team, the Minnesota Wild, was visiting Russia. The scout was ready to return home, but the air was filled with smoke from forest fires. The scout's plane could not take off.

He stayed in Russia for an extra three days. During that time, he learned about Kirill. After the scout got back to Minnesota, he told the Wild all about Kirill.

Kirill's hockey career took another leap forward in 2015. He began playing in a professional league called the Kontinental Hockey League (KHL).

In June, he was drafted by the Minnesota Wild. Kirill's hard work, determination, and a bit of luck had paid off.

Unfortunately, he could not yet begin his career in the NHL. He had already signed a contract to play for Metallurg Novokuznetsk in the KHL.

The Wild would have to wait for the young star. Kirill promised to play out his contract in Russia before coming to Minnesota.

Because he stayed in Russia, Kirill got to spend more time with his family. They celebrated his success. In five years, Kirill would achieve his dream to play in the NHL.

In the meantime, Kirill became a top player and a fan favorite in the KHL.

In 2018–2019, he led the KHL with 30 goals and helped his team win the league championship. During the next season, he became the youngest KHL player ever to reach 100 career goals.

Kirill earned a spot on the 2018 Russian Men's Olympic Ice Hockey Team. During the Olympics, he scored five goals, tied for the most by a men's player that year.

In the Gold Medal Game, Kirill's team trailed, 3–2.

Kirill assisted on a goal that tied the game. In overtime, he scored the winning goal! It was an amazing day for the team's youngest player. Kirill helped his team with all four of their points. He had three assists and one goal.

In 2020, Kirill was finally able to begin his career in the NHL. He signed a contract to play left wing for the Minnesota Wild.

He played his first NHL game on January 14, 2021, against the Los Angeles Kings. Kirill wanted to make a big impact, and he did. He assisted on a goal early in the game, and he added another assist in the third period.

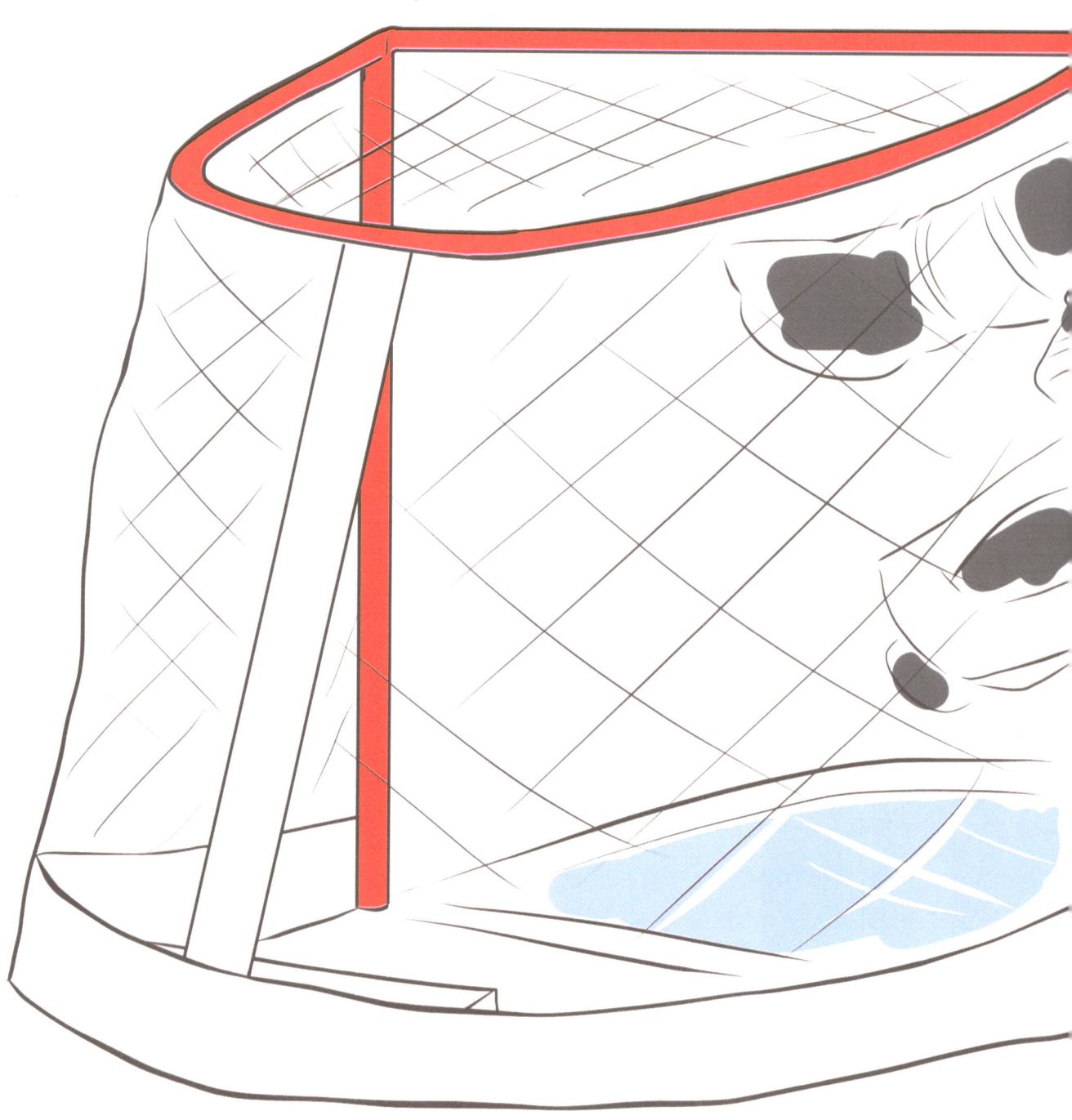

The game went into overtime, tied 3–3. Kirill stole the puck from the Kings, sped toward the net, and scored his first NHL goal to win the game! He became the only player ever to score three points (one goal, two assists) with an overtime goal in his first NHL game.

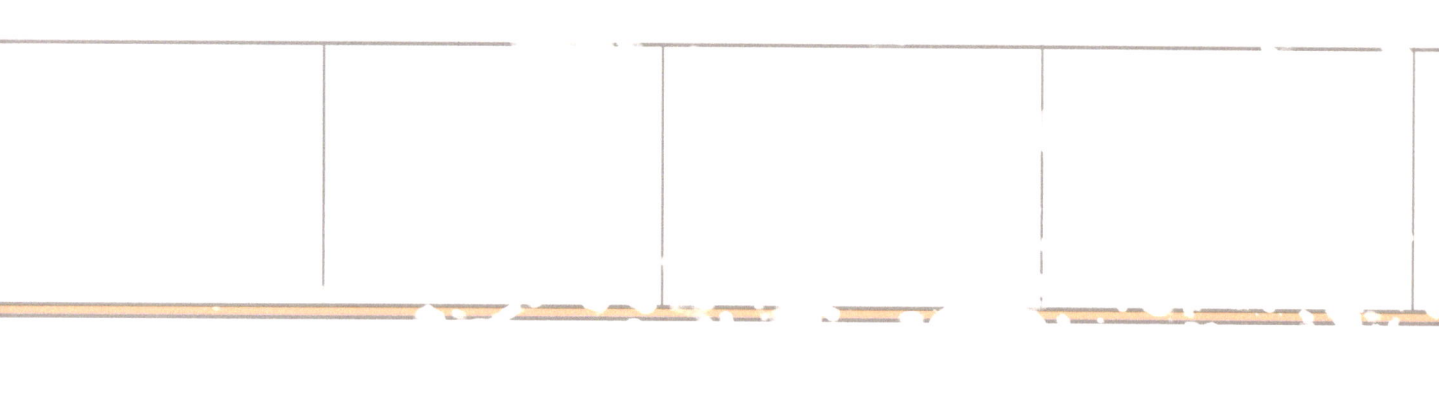

Kirill became a superstar in his second year. He was named to the NHL All-Star Game. His parents flew from Russia to see him play in person. He finished the 2021–2022 season with 47 goals and 61 assists, for a total of 108 points. All three totals were new Wild records.

The following season, he set a team record by scoring at least one goal or assist in 14 straight games. His stellar play earned him another trip to the All-Star Game. Plus, for a third time, he led the Wild into the playoffs.

As a child, Kirill dreamed big. Many believed his dreams were impossible. Kirill proved that anything can be done if a person is willing to work hard and never give up. From a small village in Russia, Kirill traveled a long way to make his dreams come true. He become one of the top players in the NHL.

ABOUT THE CREATIVE TEAM

Chad Israelson grew up in Minnesota and began following the Minnesota Vikings at five years old. For the past 25 years, Chad has been a history instructor at Rochester Community and Technical College in southeast Minnesota, winning Outstanding Educator twice and serving as faculty president for six years. In addition, he taught history courses for Augsburg and Winona State universities. Chad serves as a political analyst for KTTC, Rochester's NBC-affiliated television station, and he was a columnist for Rochester's *Post-Bulletin*. Chad is an author of various Minnesota sports books. He lives in La Crescent, Minnesota, with his wife. They have raised two sons.

Phil Juliano lives in Minnesota's Twin Cities, creating delightful illustrations for corporations, publishers, magazines, and more. He is a member of the National Cartoonists Society, and he is the creator of the syndicated comic strip *Best in Show*. When he is not drawing, he can usually be found outside somewhere, seeking his zen.

SOURCES

Schedules, statistics, and scores found at
· HockeyDB (hockeydb.com)
· Hockey Reference (hockey-reference.com).

Heckmann, Aaron. "Wild superstar Kirill Kaprizov continues to display complete package." *The Hockey News* (thehockeynews.com). June 14, 2023.

"Kirill Kaprizov" 24celebs.com (24smi.org). Accessed October 21, 2023.

"Kirill Kaprizov." Minnesota Wild (nhl.com/wild). Accessed October 21, 2023.

"Kirill Kaprizov." Players Bio (playersbio.com). Accessed October 21, 2023.

"Kirill Kaprizov." Sports Forecaster (sportsforecaster.com). Accessed October 21, 2023.

"Kuznetskie Medvedi - all time regular season player stats." Elite Hockey Prospects (eliteprospects.com). Accessed October 21, 2023.

Minnesota Wild. "Becoming Wild: Kirill Kaprizov." YouTube (youtube.com). April 9, 2021.

National Hockey League (NHL). "Kaprizov steals and scores his 1st NHL goal in OT." YouTube (youtube.com). January 14, 2021.

Potts, Andy. "Kaprizov lives up to the hype." International Ice Hockey Federation (iihf.com). January 15, 2021.

Milton Keynes UK
Ingram Content Group UK Ltd.
UKHW050213211123
432958UK00003B/88

9 781960 084309